CHRISTMAS SURPRISE
by
Cynthia Holt Cummings

illustrated by
Danna Clark

ABOUT THE AUTHOR

Cynthia Holt Cummings, a resident of West Bloomfield, Michigan was born in West Boylston, Massachusetts. Upon graduation from Massachusetts General Hospital School for Nurses, she joined the hospital's 6th General Hospital reserve unit as a second lieutenant in the Army Nurse Corps. Shortly after World War II began, the hospital unit departed for active duty, spending thirty-three months in North Africa and Italy.

She later married Richard Howe Cummings. Their son, Roger Holt Cummings, named after her youngest brother, an Air Force gunner killed during the war, is married to Buff with three children . . . David, Julie and Jessica.

ABOUT THE ARTIST

Danna Mertz Clark was born and raised in Adams County, Colorado. Her early interest in art was greatly supported by her parents, and further developed with a fondly remembered high school teacher.

She makes her home and studio on a horse farm in Oxford, Michigan, with her husband Don and five year old son Sean. Weekends are shared with step children, Cassidy and Erin.

Cynthia and Danna
dedicate this book to
our own teddy bears,

Dick and Don

and to the newest
Cummings grandchild,

 Jessica

Copyright 1985, Holt Peterson Press
Printed in the United States
First printing 1985

Holt Peterson Press
P.O. Box 3354
Farmington Hills, MI 48018

Other books by Holt Peterson Press:

CHRISTMAS LOVE
first printing 1984
second printing 1985

CHRISTMAS MEMORIES
first printing 1982

CHRISTMAS RIBBONS
first printing 1979
second printing 1980
third printing 1981
fourth printing 1982
fifth printing 1983

All rights reserved, including the right to reproduce this book, or parts thereof, in any form, except for the inclusion of brief quotations in a review.

Who would ever believe that a family of bears
Would live in a house with circular stairs?

Surprise was the Master of them all
Living in the closet in the upstairs hall.

L.C.B. at the foot of the stairs
Commanded respect from all of the bears.

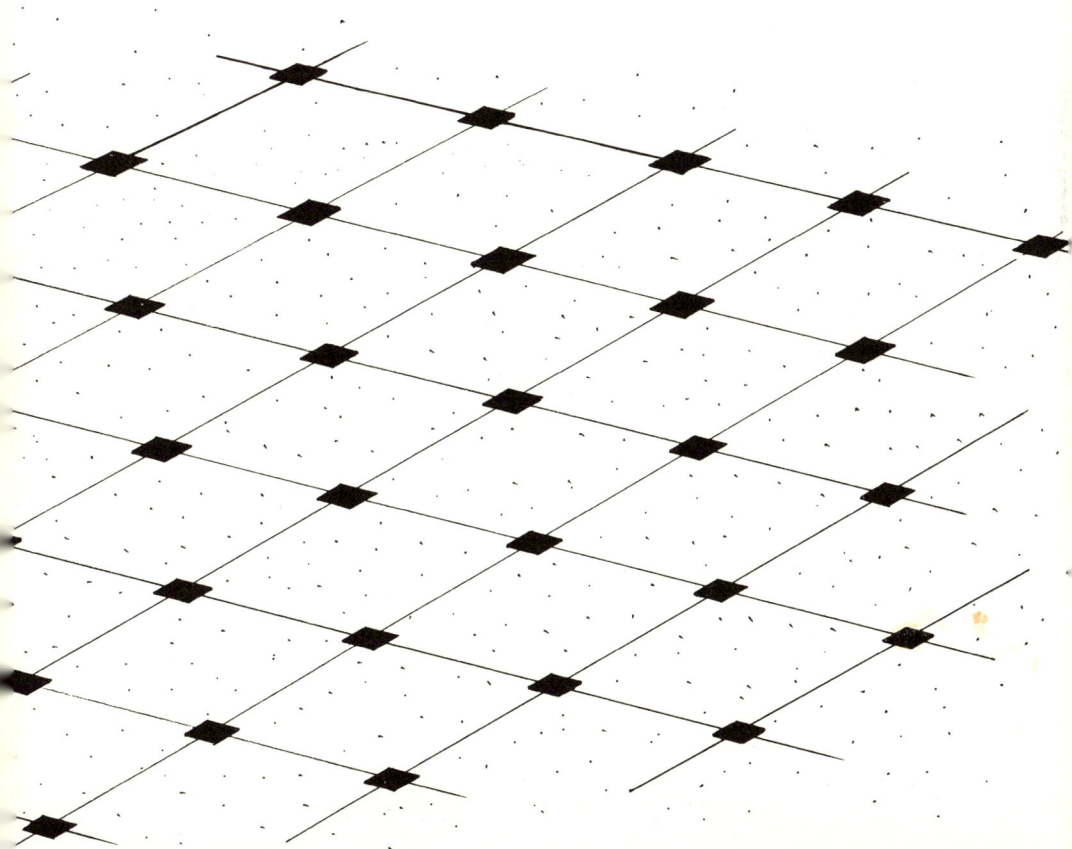

Patchwork with his out-stretched arms
Welcomed Mandy with all her charms.

And as the days would come and go
The family of bears would grow and grow.

Mr. Brag and Camelot,

Muffy and Fluffy

and ForGetMeNot.

When Prince William arrived
He caused quite a stir,
Because of his size and his white coat of fur.

Too big for the chair — Too big for the stair
He sat on the floor for all to adore.

Nanny was there with her get-well pills
As she soothed their brows and nursed their ills.

Grandchildren came to visit the bears,
And shared their secrets on the circular stairs.

The seasons would come with the rain and the snow,
And the flowers would bloom,
And the green trees would grow.

There were summer picnics and the patio chairs
Were just the right size for the family of bears.

And after Summer would come the Fall,
And the wind scattered leaves for Bears large and small.

The bears loved the seasons, Summer and Fall,
But looked forward to Christmas most of all.

Surprise had a plan for all of the bears
As he quickly came down the circular stairs;
In a voice that could be heard the length of the hall
Surprise said — "This will be the best Christmas —
   The best Christmas of All."

For I know, I know that Santa will take
All of the gifts that we can make
To share with others along his way
To give them a Happy Christmas Day.

What fun to listen to all the Bears talk
When Winter is covered with snow on the walk.

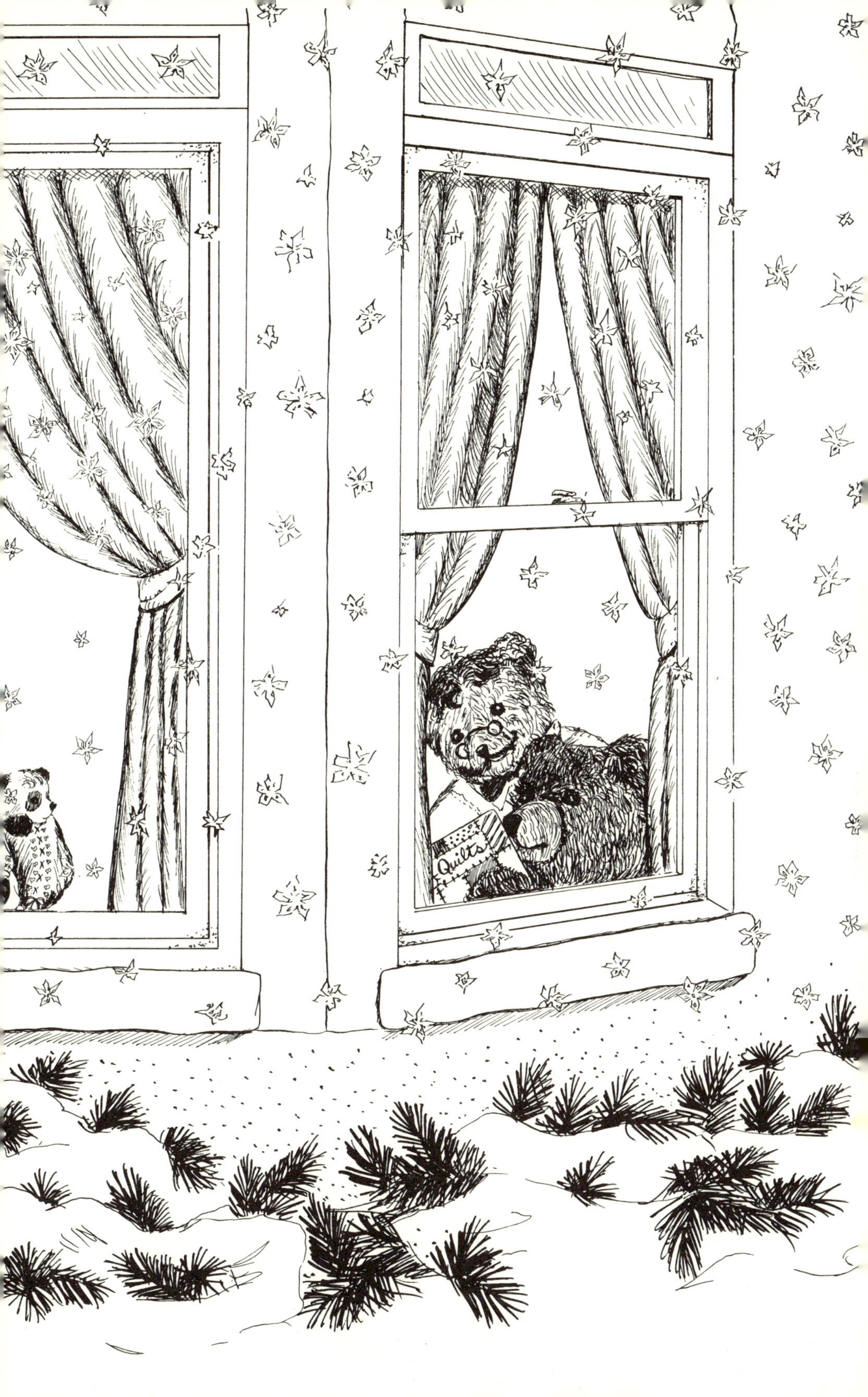
Quilts

Surrounded by pieces of ribbons red
And shiny black buttons and bright colored thread.

Pieces of silk and pieces of satin
Were cut very carefully from each little pattern.

They sketched

and they painted,

They stitched

and they pasted.

And never a minute was ever wasted.

They made quilts of small patches
With each stitch in place

And tiny doll dresses of satin and lace.

They made paper chains of red and green
And get-well cards with a Christmas scene.

They thought of the children in far away places,
And the smiles they would bring to all of their faces.

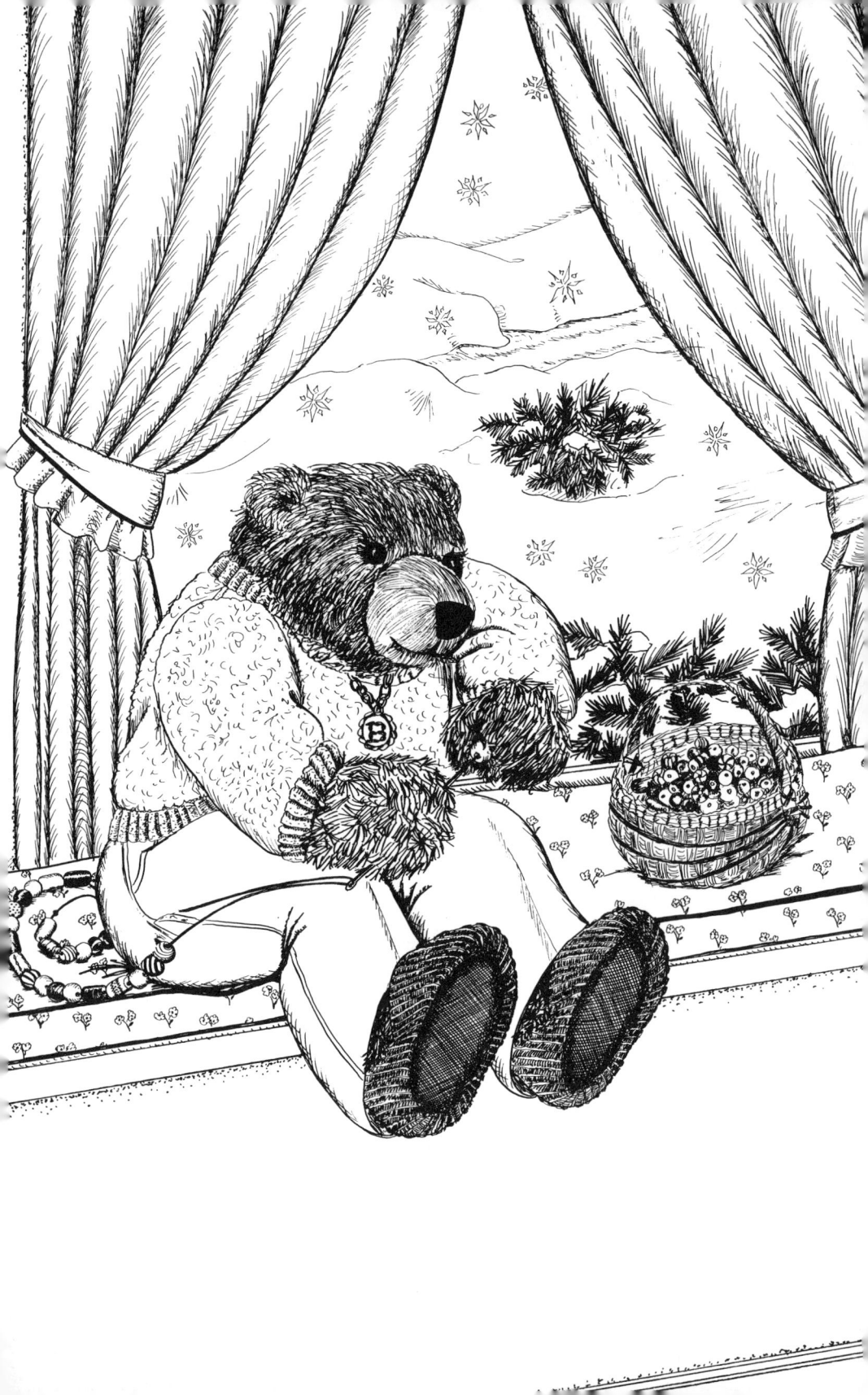

It was strange to see Brag sitting there
As quiet as any other bear
Stringing beads on a piece of string
And never bragging about a thing.

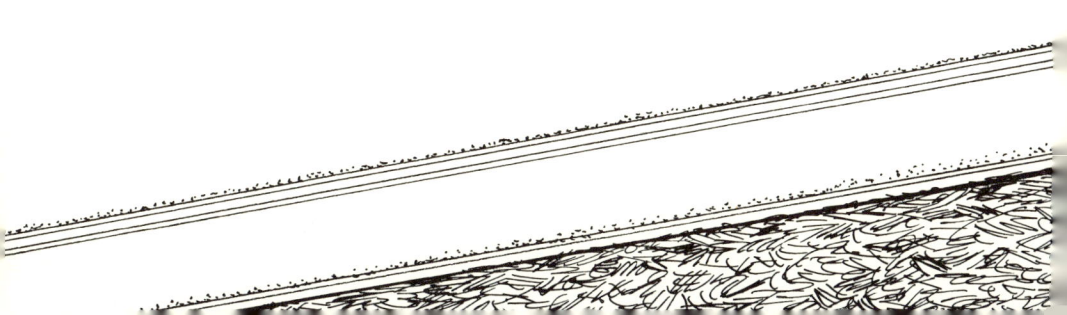

Mandy and Patchwork were busy tying tags
On home-made candy in little brown bags.

The family of bears never had such fun
Making surprises for the Christmas to come.

L.C.B. watched at the foot of the stairs
And he was so proud of that family of bears.

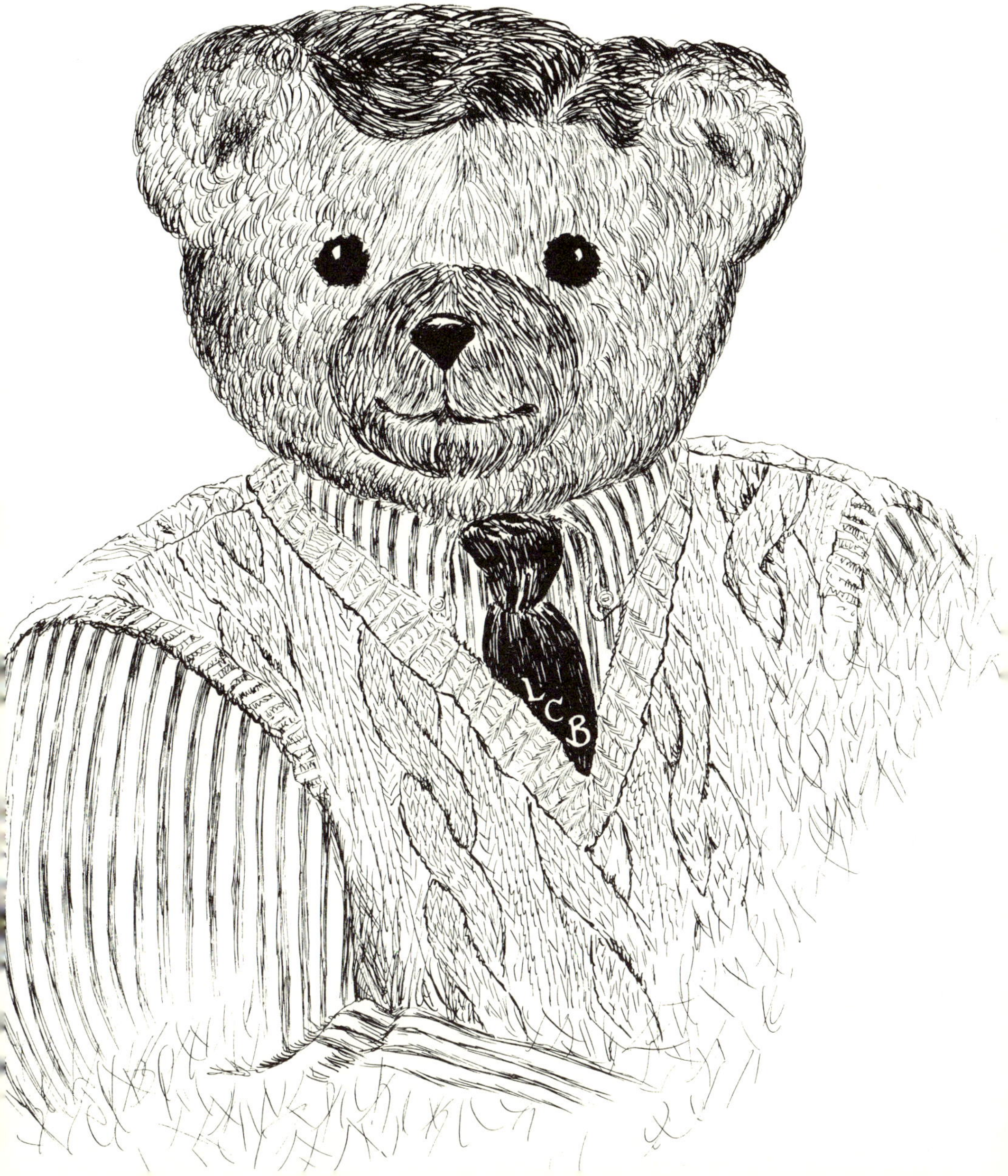
LCB

There were presents in piles all over the floor,
Prince William was surrounded like never before;

Oh, he wished that Santa would soon be there
To take all the gifts the bears made to share.

Surprise was as busy as busy could be
Trimming the Bear family Christmas tree.
He had to reach up ever so far
To the top of the tree to pin the gold star.

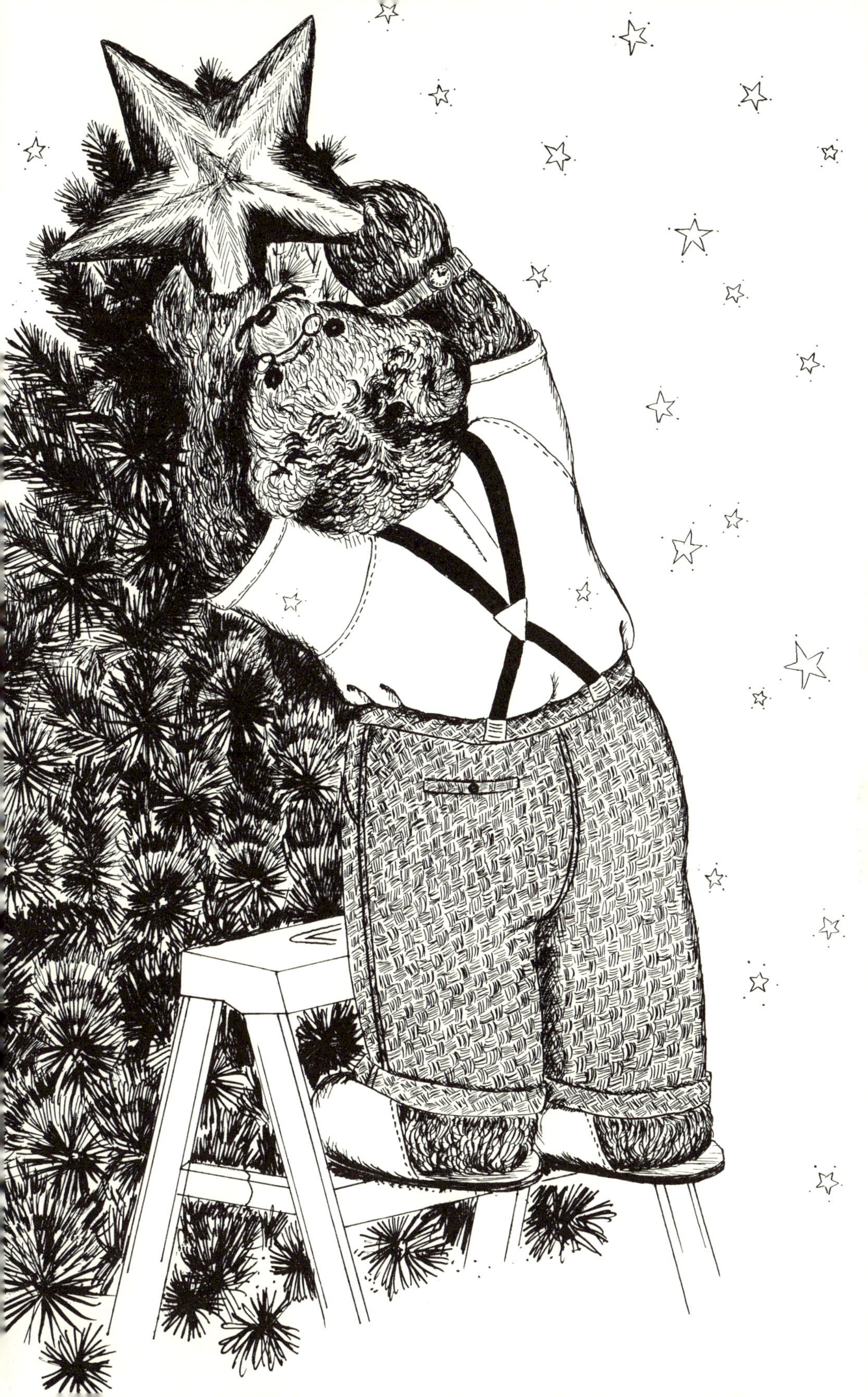

He tied on each branch red ribbon bows
And little green mittens to wear when it snows.
Bright yellow scarves for the winter wind
With a bear written tag marked only from him.

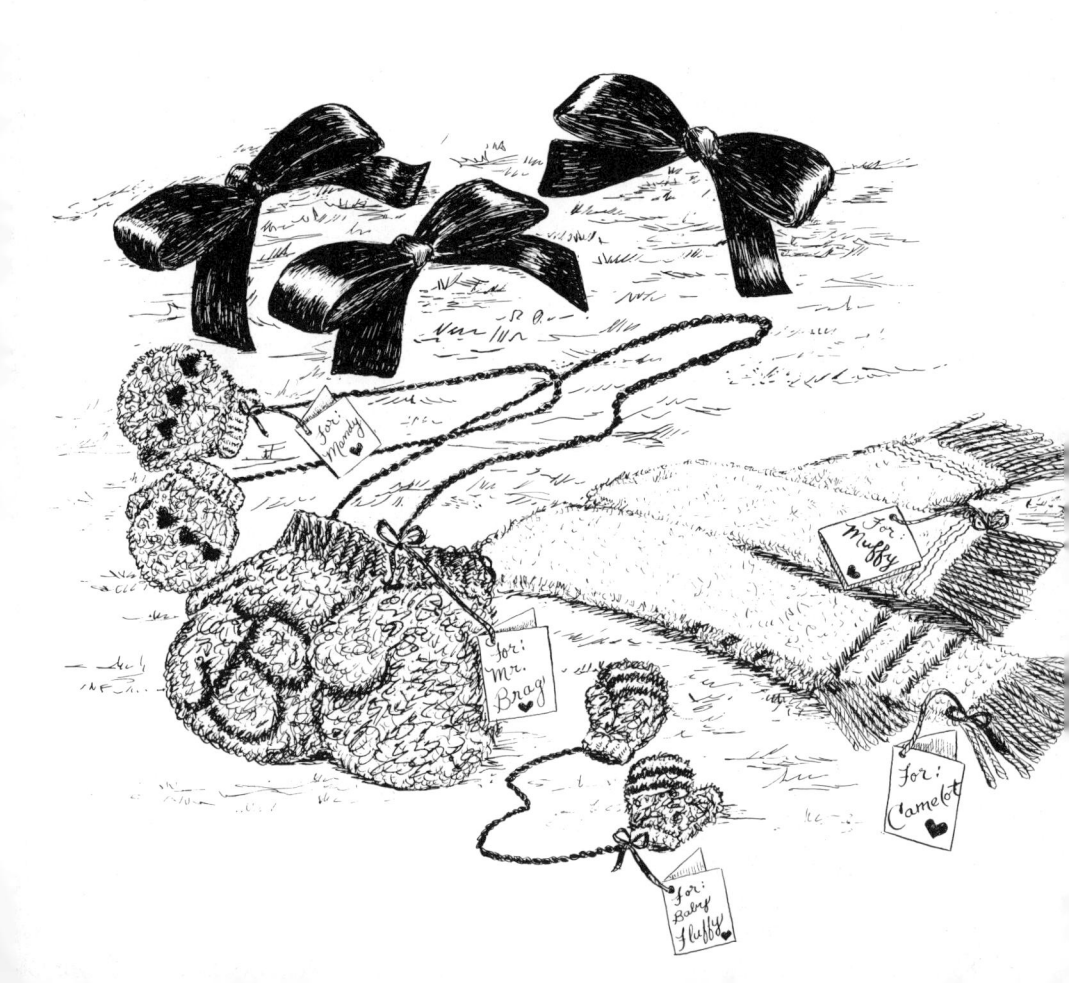

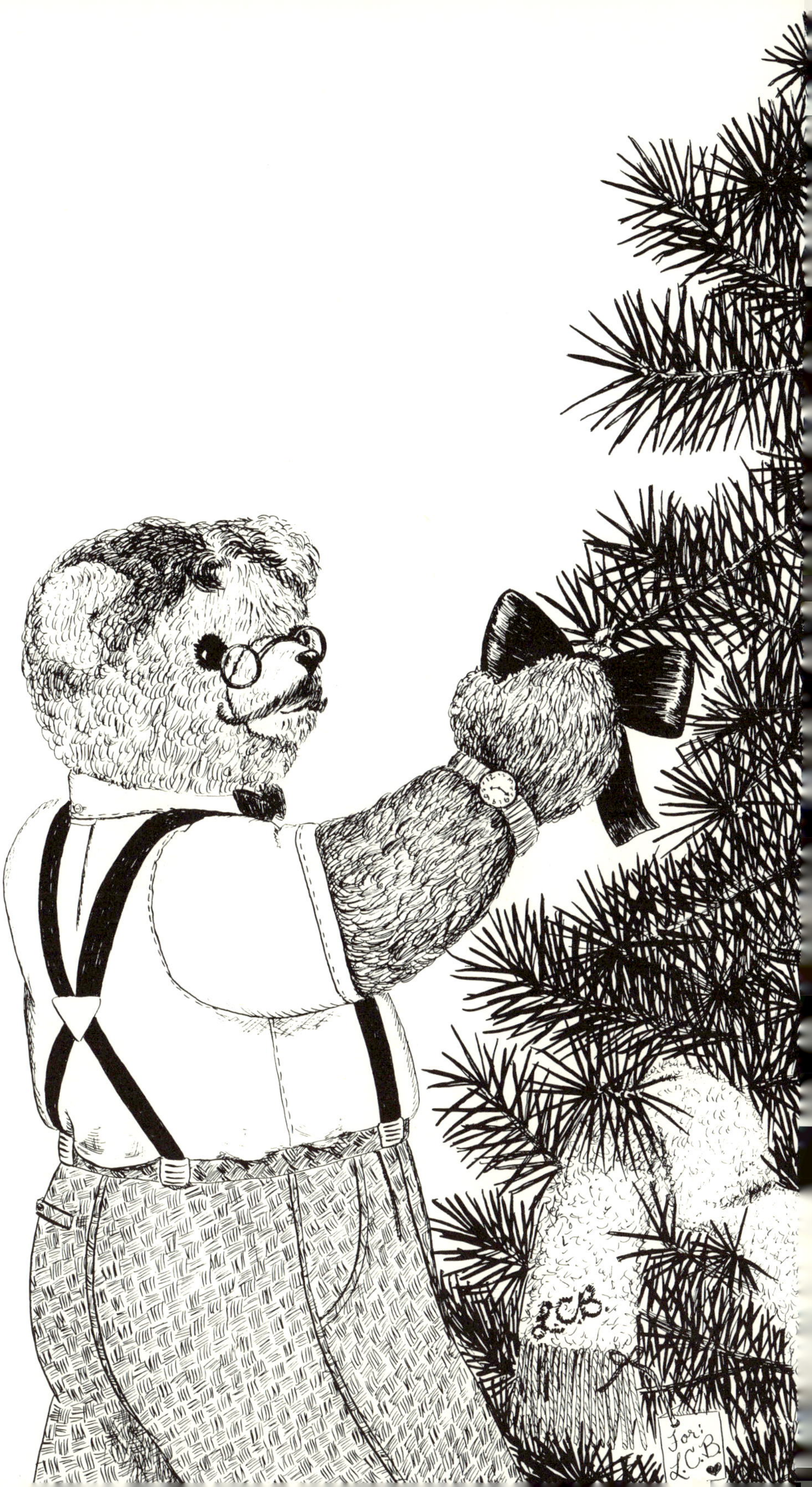

LCB.
For:
L.C.B

He sat down to rest in the living room chair
With love in his heart for each special bear.

He looked out at the fields white with snow
And the green fir trees with lights all aglow
And he wished for all a world of Peace
With love for each other that would never cease.

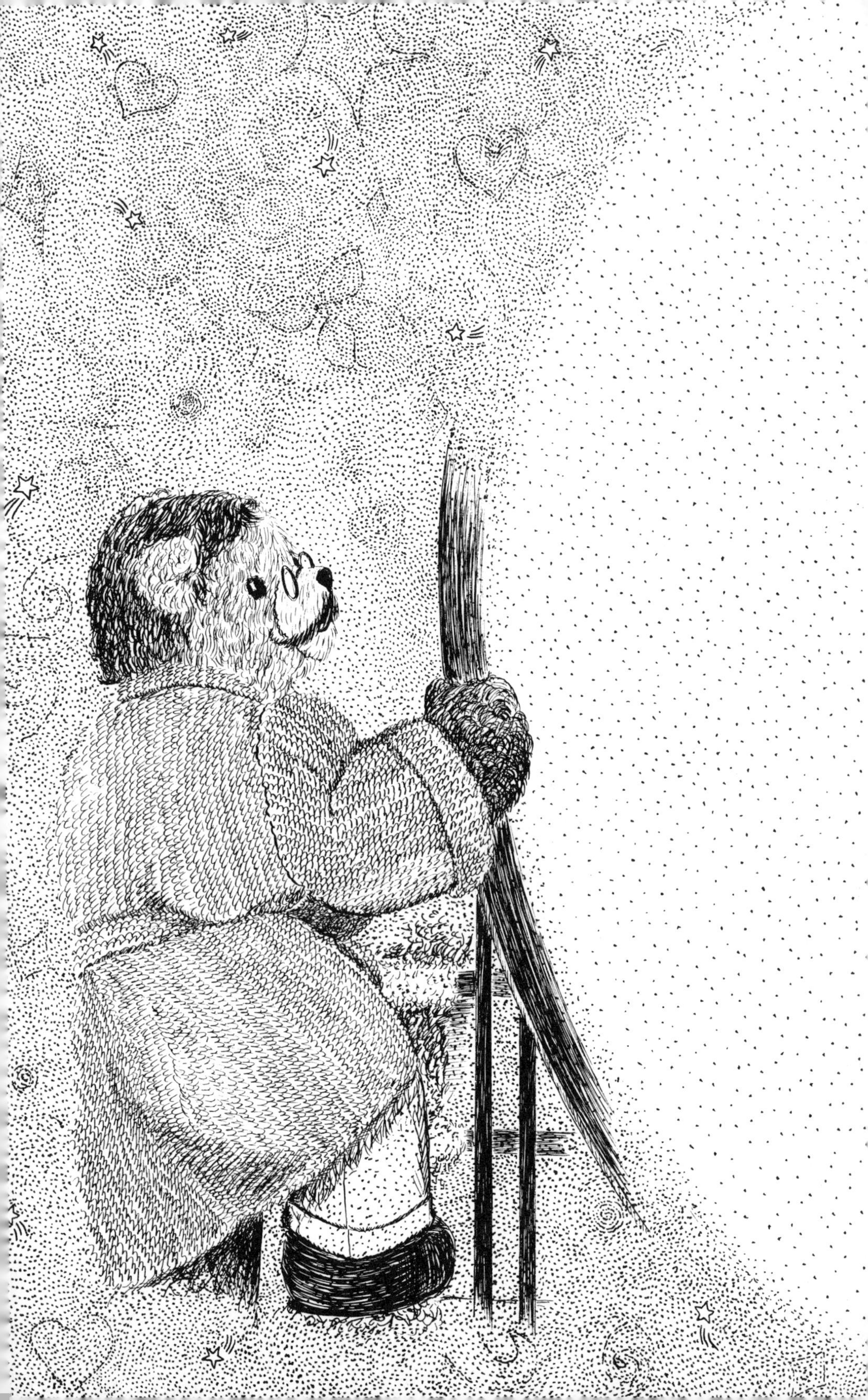

Then Surprise slowly climbed the circular stairs
And after saying goodnite to the family of bears —

He stretched out in his bed in the closet in the hall
Knowing this would be the best Christmas —
   The best Christmas of All.

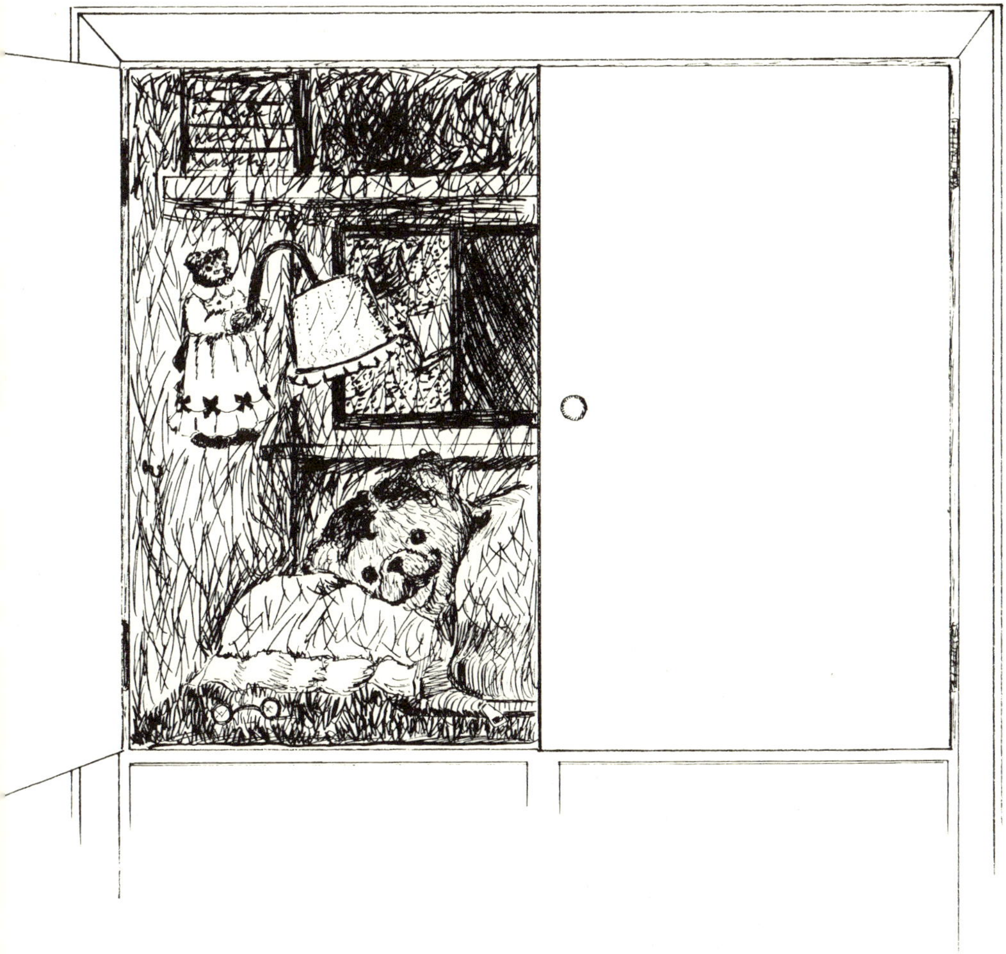

Peace filled the room this Christmas night
As a family of bears saw the star so bright
And thoughts of Love and Hope and Good Cheer
Were wished for all in the coming New Year.

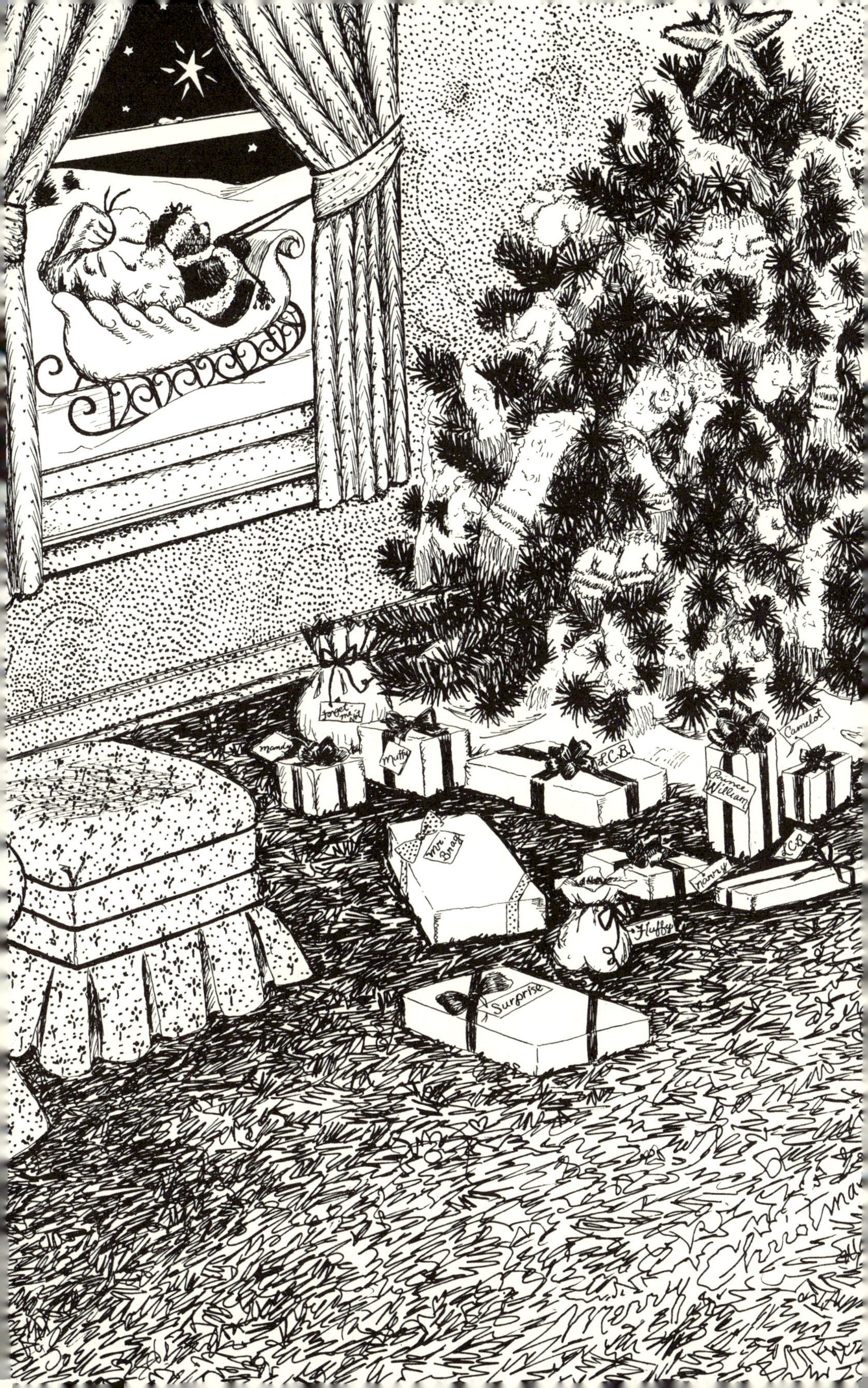

You need never be lonely
When friends fail to call
With a family of bears
To fill up the hall,

To sit in a chair,
To have afternoon tea,
To celebrate Christmas
Around a fir tree.

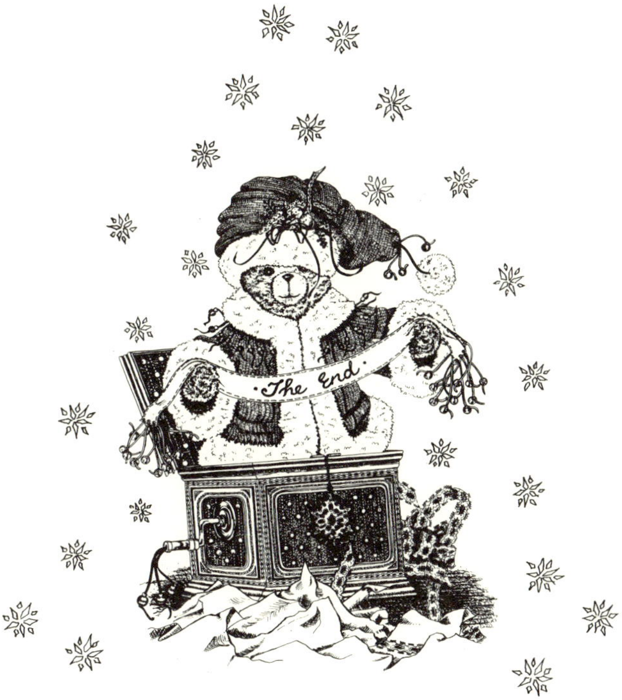
·The End·

My Christmas Memories

My Christmas Memories

My Christmas Memories

My Christmas Memories

My Christmas Memories

My Christmas Memories

My Christmas Memories

My Christmas Memories

My Christmas Memories

My Christmas Memories

My Christmas Memories

My Christmas Memories

My Christmas Memories

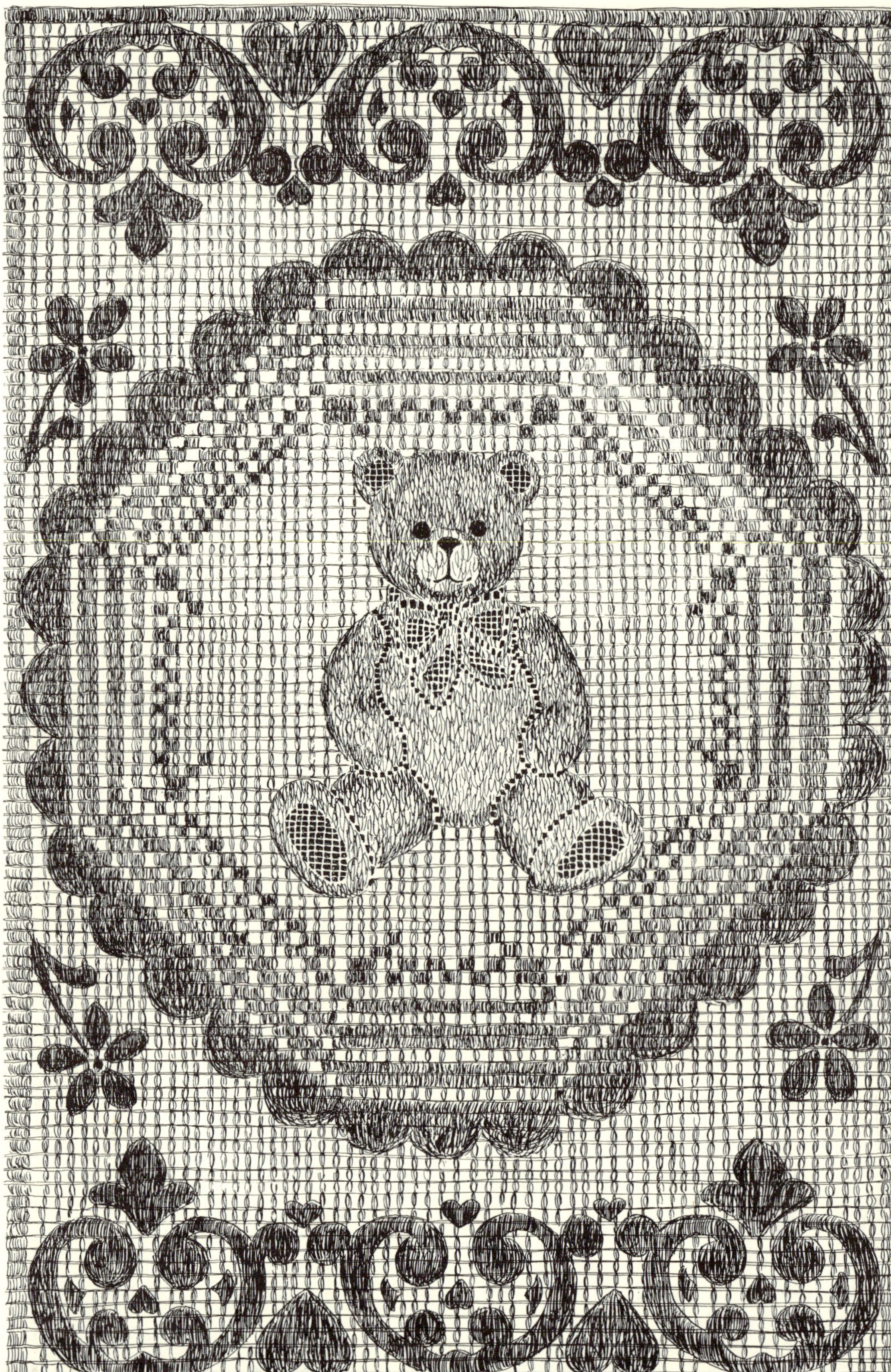